EARTH ALERT!

Settlements

Stephanie Turner

HODDER
Wayland

an imprint of Hodder Children's Books

WWF

Produced in Association with WWF UK

Earth Alert!

Coasts	Settlements
Energy	Transport
Farming	Rivers

Cover: A variety of homes in Delhi, India.
Title page: Part of Ho Chi Minh city, Vietnam.
Contents page: A town in Greece.

First published in Great Britain in 1998 by Wayland (Publishers) Ltd
Reprinted in 2000 by Hodder Wayland,
an imprint of Hodder Children's Books
© Hodder Wayland 1998

All Wayland books encourage children to read and help them improve their literacy.

✓ The contents page, page numbers, headings and index help locate specific pieces of information.

✓ The glossary reinforces alphabetic knowledge and extends vocabulary.

✓ The further information section suggests other books dealing with the same subject.

WWF UK is a registered charity no. 201707
WWF UK, Panda House, Weyside Park, Godalming,
Surrey GU7 1XR

British Library Cataloguing in Publication Data
Turner, Stephanie
    Settlements. – (Earth alert)
    1. Human settlements – Juvenile literature 2. Land
    settlement – Juvenile literature 3. Human Settlements –
    Environmental aspects – Juvenile literature 4. Land
    settlement – Environmental aspects – Juvenile literature.
    I. Title
    307.1'4

ISBN 0 7502 2261 1

Designed by Gus Ferguson
Printed and bound in Italy by Eurografica, Italy

This book was prepared for
Wayland Publishers Ltd by
Margot Richardson,
23 Hanover Terrace, Brighton, E Sussex, BN2 2SN

Picture acknowledgements
Alphen aan den Rijn Information 29; Axiom Photographic
Agency 17 (Jim Holmes); James Davis Travel Photography 7;
Eye Ubiquitous 18 (Paul Hutley), 21 and 24 (Paul Thompson);
Getty Images 1 (Jerry Alexander), 4 (Michel Setboun), 5
(Oliver Benn), 10 (Nicholas DeVore), 11 (Sue Cunningham),
16 (Jeremy Walker), 20 (Johan Elzenga), 25 (Robert A
Mitchell), 27 (David Hanover); Impact Photos 8
(Mark Henley), 9 (Mark Henley), 12 (Alan Keohane),13
(Mark Henley), 15 (Sergio Dorantes), 22 (David Silverberg), 23
(Philip Gordon), 28 (Mark Henley); Alex Robb 6 (both);
Stephanie Turner 26 (both); Wayland Picture Library 3 (Julia
Waterlow), 14, 19. Dustbin information on page 19 courtesy
of Ecoschools, Tidy Britain Group.
Artwork by Peter Bull Art Studio.

find Wayland on the Internet at http://www.wayland.co.uk

Author's acknowledgement
For my parents,
Mary and Allan Rodley,
who first encouraged my
interest in the environment.

Contents

Where People Live

Where do people live? Where do you live? In a flat or a house; in the country or a town? Most people in the world live in groups – of tents, huts, houses or flats. We call these groups settlements.

In the countryside the settlements are small, from a few houses in a hamlet to 20 to 200 houses in a village. These are called rural settlements. Large numbers of houses and other buildings are called towns, and bigger groups still are cities. These are urban settlements.

In order to live, people need food and a supply of fresh water. They also need shelter, so they must have materials for building. Fuels are also necessary for cooking and heating.

Some people live in settlements of tents or huts. This is so they can move around. These people are called nomads.

The development of settlements

Gradually, people built their homes closer together in larger groups. Sometimes they had to defend their homes against enemies. These people built settlements on hills or steep river banks, and added walls or ditches to keep other people out.

Towns grew up on transport routes, and where people could trade with each other. Farmers could sell the things they grew but did not need, and buy things they could not make themselves, such as salt. Towns with markets and shops developed where it was easy for people to meet: on crossroads, rivers, and later, beside railways.

Other towns have developed because they have special purposes. Ports on coasts and rivers are where boats and ships load or unload. Industrial towns are where large numbers of people work in factories.

A castle in Segovia, a walled town in Spain.

Types of settlement

The size of a settlement is measured by how many people live there, not the area of land it is built on.

Hamlet	Fewer than 50 people: a few houses and farms.
Village	50 to 1,000 people: houses, farms, a church and perhaps one or two shops.
Town	1,000 to 100,000 people: houses, churches, shops, factories, offices, banks.
City	100,000 to millions of people: houses, churches, shops, factories, offices, banks, perhaps a university and government offices.

A farming settlement

In many parts of the world, groups of people live on or near their farms. In the village of Kenari, on the Indonesian island of Flores, most of the people are farmers. They grow rice in nearby paddy fields, using water buffalo to plough the land.

Raising houses up on stilts makes the houses cool, and keeps people safe from wild animals.

Houses are built from local materials, mostly bamboo and rattan (palm stems). As the climate is hot, the houses are raised up high on stilts to let air flow underneath to cool them. In the village there are a school, a post office and a small shop.

There is no electricity in Kenari, so people use oil lamps for light at night, and they cook over open fires. Water comes from a nearby river. People either grow their own food, or buy from a market, 13 km away. There is no transport to the market: people must walk there and back.

There are many villages like Kenari on the islands of Indonesia, but also some larger settlements with modern homes.

The children who live in Kenari go to the village school.

6

Settlements and landscape

The natural environment has influenced the location of many settlements. For example, some are in places where the land is flat. Others are built around harbours where it is safe for ships to anchor. It is hard to build settlements, or to grow food, on steep mountains, sandy deserts or in very cold areas. So, not many people live there.

Settlements also affect the landscape around them. People change the environment by chopping down trees, moving earth and covering the land with buildings and roads. They may also pollute the land, water and air with their rubbish and other waste products.

New York grew up on an island at the mouth of the Hudson River. The river has been badly polluted because of the huge number of people living nearby.

Cities can be so crowded that some people must live in very small homes.

Settlements today

People still have the basic needs of water, food and shelter. They also need energy for light, cooking and warmth, and some way of getting rid of their waste. All over the world, more and more people are living in towns and cities. This is because there is usually more work there than in the country, and probably because there are more things to do.

Towns and cities are getting bigger all the time. This is because the population of the world is growing, and because more people are moving to live in urban areas. Some cities contain millions of people. As cities have become more busy and crowded, there is less land to go round. Some city dwellers have to live in very small homes.

World's Largest Cities (1996)	
	millions of people
Tokyo, Japan	27.0
Mexico City, Mexico	16.6
São Paulo, Brazil	16.5
New York, USA	16.3
Bombay, India	15.1
Shanghai, China	13.6
Los Angeles, USA	12.4
Calcutta, India	12.0
Buenos Aires, Argentina	11.8
Seoul, South Korea	11.6

Activity

Your settlement: how has it changed?

Visit your local library or museum to look at maps of your home area. Find a historical map of how the area used to be, and one from the present day. Compare them to see how your area has changed.

- Which is the earliest map? Is there a date on it?
- Was the settlement smaller or bigger in those days?
- Can you work out why the settlement began there?
- What are the differences between now and the past?

A new office block and old houses exist side by side in Shanghai, China.

Because settlements are getting bigger all the time, they are always changing. Buildings wear out or are no longer big enough, so they are altered, or knocked down and new ones are put up. The new buildings are often bigger or taller than the older ones. More roads are built, widened or altered. As a result, overcrowding and pollution are common.

There are many environmental problems in settlements, but also many interesting ways of dealing with them.

Shelter and Buildings

People need shelter to protect them from the weather: wind, rain, strong sunlight and cold temperatures. Many thousands of years ago, people lived in caves or trees. Gradually, they learned to build homes or shelters.

Local materials

Houses in Lesotho, Africa. They are made from local stone, earth and wood.

At first, huts were built from local materials such as wood, clay and stone. Many people, especially in small settlements, live in homes made just from what they can find around them. Sometimes there is no wood nearby, so homes must be made of stone and earth. In other places, there are lots of trees, so all the homes are made from wood.

Finding somewhere to live

All round the world there are people who find it hard to get somewhere to live.

Some leave the countryside because they do not have any work, or do not own land to grow food. They come to cities to look for work, but cannot find anywhere to live, usually because they do not have much money. They build huts from whatever they can find, such as bits of wood and sheets of metal or plastic. These people live on the poorest land, often steep hillsides, without electricity or running water. The huts grow into shanty towns. These can be found on the edges of big cities all over the world, but especially in Asia, Africa and South America.

In many cities, very poor people live in one area, while rich people live in another, often in big houses behind high walls and locked gates.

A shanty town, on the edge of Rio de Janeiro in Brazil, overlooks modern blocks of flats.

Buildings and the environment

Modern buildings are made from many different materials: wood, stone, brick, cement, metal, glass and plastic. These materials may travel many kilometres from where they are made. They are transported on lorries, trains and ships.

Finding, making and moving materials has a direct effect on the environment. Sometimes whole hillsides are dug up or quarried to find stone, and forests are chopped down for wood. Factories making cement, glass or plastic use up energy and produce smoke. Lorries pollute the air with their fumes.

Energy

Everyone needs energy. In settlements we use it for cooking, lighting, heating water, keeping warm, making things cool, transport, and power for machines, from a kitchen toaster to huge factory machines. Energy comes from many sources. Those used most at present are wood, coal, gas, oil, nuclear and water power.

Using energy

In some villages, people gather wood and cook their food over an open fire. They may not have electricity, and so cannot use lights at night or machines such as refrigerators or televisions.

People who use wood for cooking and heat usually have to gather it themselves.

People in towns and cities use huge quantities of energy in the form of electricity, gas and oil. There are lights in homes, offices and streets. People cook using electricity or gas. They use electricity to run many machines, such as computers, stereos and washing machines.

Problems with energy

Wood can be replaced by planting more trees. However, there is not enough coal, oil and gas to last for ever. If we keep burning these fuels at the same rate as now, they will completely run out.

Coal, oil and natural gas are all fuels which are burnt to produce energy, and to make electricity. The burning releases smoke and gases into the atmosphere. These are known as 'greenhouse gases' as they keep the sun's warmth on the earth. Many scientists believe that the large amounts of fuels being burned are leading to a small, gradual rise in temperatures all over the world. This may cause problems in the future.

Burning these fuels and using petrol in cars and buses causes air pollution. The fumes in the atmosphere are unpleasant for people who live and work in cities. The fumes make some illnesses worse, and it can be hard for some people to breathe.

Cities and towns have busy streets. They are often congested with cars and buses, all burning petrol to make them move.

Food

People need land on which to grow food. Crops are grown in fields. Animals graze on grass or are kept in large buildings. Most villages, towns and cities are made up of buildings grouped closely together, so there is not enough space to grow much food nearby. Therefore food has to be brought into settlements from outside. Food is grown in rural areas and is transported into urban areas.

Transporting food

In wealthy countries, some food is transported over long distances. This is because people want to eat a variety of food all year round. They also want to eat foreign foods that do not grow in their own country.

Transporting food for many kilometres before it reaches the shops affects the environment, both in the country and in towns. Roads are busy with many lorries, some of which are refrigerated to keep the food fresh. This uses up much fuel, and also causes air pollution. Some food is even transported by plane, which causes even more waste of resources and pollution.

Oranges grow only in warm countries. They travel long distances to reach some shops.

Patterns of shopping

Thirty or forty years ago, people would visit small shops or markets to buy their food, often in the town centre. Since then, food shops have grown bigger and bigger, and some supermarkets are now very large.

Some towns and cities were built with narrow roads and small buildings. Large supermarkets take up a lot of space and have big car parks. To find this space, new supermarkets have been built on the outskirts of towns.

A huge shopping centre in Mexico. People depend on cars to get to 'out-of-town' shops.

Activity

Where does your food come from?

Collect a variety of food labels that show where the food was produced: that is the country of origin. Try to find as many labels as possible, all from different countries. Use an atlas to find out where the countries are. On an outline world map stick the labels or draw pictures of the foods on the countries where they are grown.

Draw lines from the country where the food was grown to your own home. Measure the distance to see how far your food has travelled to your plate. Does food need to travel that far? Why?

Water

People cannot live without safe drinking water. Settlements cannot exist unless they have a reliable supply of water nearby.

Average water use

Cleaning teeth	2 litres
Washing hands	0.6 litres
Flushing a toilet	9.5 litres
Taking a shower	35 litres
Dishwasher cycle	55 litres
Taking a bath	80 litres
Washing machine cycle	110 litres
Watering garden with a sprinkler	10 litres per minute
Drinking and Cooking	10 litres per person per day

To have water available all the time, towns and cities have to store it in large amounts. Sometimes it is stored in reservoirs. Other places get their supplies from water that has seeped into rock underground. The water is piped into people's homes. On the way, it passes through treatment works to make sure it is safe to drink.

In some places, dirty water and sewage pass straight into rivers or the sea. This can cause diseases and kill wildlife.

After the water has been used, it is piped to sewage works to be treated, so that it can be safely returned to rivers or to the sea.

Water for everyone

Some places have plenty of water, while others do not have enough. In many countries, rainfall is low and people have to make do with a small amount of water. Others may have to travel long distances to the nearest river or well, and then walk back to their village carrying the water, which is very heavy.

Most people in towns and cities take water for granted. Because water is there when they turn on a tap, they do not think about how much they use. Some people use too much water, and the level of water in rivers and under the ground is going down faster than it can be replaced by nature. We must make sure we store and use water carefully so that there will be enough for everyone.

A boy in Bangladesh carries drinking water from a well to his home.

Activity

How much water do you use?

Use the information in the Fact Box on page 16 to work out how much water your family uses in one day.

- How much water can you carry at a time?
- How many journeys would you have to make if you were responsible for fetching all your family's water?
- How might you try to make the job easier?

Waste

People everywhere produce all kinds of waste products, including sewage and solid rubbish. When a large number of people live together in a settlement, getting rid of waste becomes a big problem because there is so much in one area.

Getting rid of waste

Most settlements are organized to get rid of waste. Large pipes called sewers take away dirty water and sewage. Some places have treatment works, where the water is cleaned. In other places, the waste runs straight into rivers or the sea.

Solid waste is taken to rubbish dumps where it is burned or buried in the ground. However, while burying hides the rubbish, it does not make it go away. Some waste, such as plastic, never rots and stays in the ground for ever.

Throwing away rubbish can damage the land, the air or the water, and this is called pollution. Rubbish dumps and waste water can also be places where diseases live. If rubbish is not disposed of safely, people may become ill and some may die.

Bulldozers are used to spread out rubbish and cover it with earth.

Recycling

People have become concerned about pollution and what to do with waste, especially in cities. They are trying to find ways of dealing with waste that are better than burning or burying it.

One suggestion is to recycle as many things as possible. This means changing waste into things that can be used again. Paper, glass, plastics, aluminium, tin cans and clothes may all be recycled. Perhaps we should try to use less in the first place.

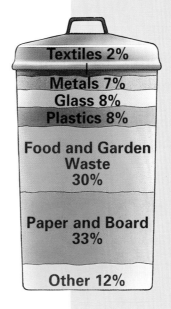

What is in your dustbin?

Textiles 2%
Metals 7%
Glass 8%
Plastics 8%
Food and Garden Waste 30%
Paper and Board 33%
Other 12%

This is what an average household dustbin contains in a wealthy country such as the UK, USA, Australia or Canada.

This means that up to 88 per cent of household waste could be recycled.

CASE STUDY

Recycling in Florida

Like many modern cities, Fort Lauderdale in southern Florida, in the USA, operates a recycling programme. Every household is offered a special bin, free of charge. People put their recyclable rubbish in the bins which are collected and emptied once a week.

The city also operates a 'Trash Transfer Station' and a 'Bulk Trash Pick Up Program' for large items of rubbish that can be recycled, such as old furniture, garden waste and tyres.

The rubbish department does not stop there. It also runs a group called the 'Recycle Corps' which is made up of ordinary people who live in the city. The Corps has come up with a city-wide logo and information to encourage all the residents of Fort Lauderdale to recycle as much as possible.

Many towns now have a collection service for any rubbish that can be recycled.

Work and Play

In rural areas, people mainly work as farmers or in businesses that are related to farming. In towns and cities there are many more offices and factories providing a wide variety of jobs.

Zones

As towns and cities have grown, so different parts have developed special uses. These parts of big settlements are called zones or areas.

Industrial areas and homes may be in separate parts of a town. It is not pleasant to live near smoke or noise.

In one part of a town you will find the shops, banks and offices where people work. This is called a commercial zone. In another part there may be factories and workshops. This area is called an industrial zone. And another part of town is mostly houses and flats. This is known as a residential area.

Travelling

Some people travel long distances each day to reach their work. This is because they live in one part of a settlement and work in another. These people are called commuters. Towns and cities are very busy in the rush hour each morning and evening. This is when commuters enter and leave by bus, train, car and bicycle.

All this travel, especially by car, causes air and noise pollution, which may make life very unpleasant for people who live near busy roads.

In most towns and cities there is not enough road space for people to drive into the centre, and nowhere for them to park when they get there. People are encouraged to use public transport, such as trains, trams and buses. These carry many people at the same time and do not need space to park. This helps to reduce pollution in urban environments.

Commuters cross a bridge in London, on their way to work. Trains and buses bring them into the city from residential areas.

Leisure and play

Everyone needs a chance to relax after work or school. In towns and cities, there is not much room for open space, but most settlements have public places for relaxation. These may be parks, playgrounds, sports fields, swimming pools, leisure centres, cinemas and theatres.

Urban parks and open spaces make settlements more pleasant for people to live in. They also provide habitats for plants and animals.

Central Park, in the middle of New York, is quiet and peaceful.

Tokyo is the world's largest city. It has spread out over a huge area of land.

Planning

As towns have become busy and crowded there has been competition for land. Some far-sighted people have decided to plan towns in an organized way rather than just let them grow and spread out haphazardly.

People have different ideas about the best way to plan towns and cities. Some feel it is best for people to live near their work in large towns. This means they would have to travel less, which would save energy and reduce pollution.

Other people believe different parts of towns should be set aside for different uses. There are then separate areas for industry, housing, shopping and leisure. People may live in attractive places, but they have to travel more. Clean, cheap and reliable public transport is needed.

Change

Settlements are getting bigger all the time. This is partly because the world's population is always increasing, and partly because more and more people are crowding into towns and cities every year. Two hundred years ago, only 5 per cent of the world's people lived in towns or cities. Now more than 50 per cent live in urban environments.

An area of high-rise apartments in Hong Kong.

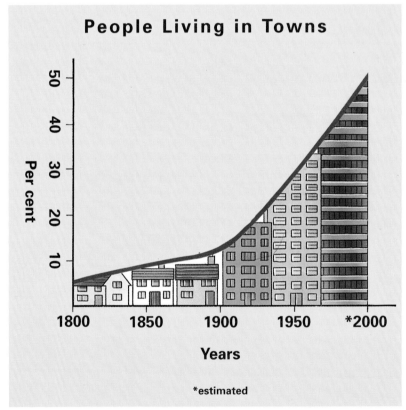

People Living in Towns

Per cent (50, 40, 30, 20, 10)

Years (1800, 1850, 1900, 1950, *2000)

*estimated

Competition for land

In many cities there is a shortage of land. As towns have become more congested, so ways of building have changed. Many people now live in 'high-rise' flats which are a way of fitting a lot of people into a small area.

'Out-of-town' development

As cities have become more congested, so out-of-town developments have occurred. 'Business parks' and 'science parks' have been built on the edge of many towns in, for example, Britain and the USA.

Here there is more space for factories, and delivery lorries do not have to drive into city centres. In some places, it may be easier to build on 'greenfield' sites. However this sort of development can lead to more travelling, more roads and towns spreading out into the countryside.

Offices built on the edges of towns may appear more pleasant than those in urban areas, but some cause environmental problems.

This may lead to problems in cities, with businesses moving out and jobs disappearing. Factories and shops close and people move away.

Redevelopment

Some parts of cities have been redeveloped. The old buildings which are no longer used have been pulled down and the area cleared. New buildings, houses, factories, offices and roads have been built, completely changing the area. Sometimes an industrial area has been cleared to make a park.

Camley Street Natural Park

Camley Street Natural Park is a nature reserve in the centre of London, the largest city in Britain. The park includes a large pond, meadows and woodland. These provide a natural environment for birds, bees, butterflies, frogs and many varieties of plants.

The area was once a storage area for coal, and later became a rubbish tip. The waste land was redeveloped to create the park, starting in 1983. All the rubbish had to be cleared away, and then the area was landscaped.

The park is surrounded by busy roads, railway lines and enormous gas holders, and it is just near a major railway station, Kings Cross. Nevertheless, it is now a haven for wildlife, and for people, right in the centre of the busy city.

Visitors are welcomed at the park. Many children from urban schools visit to study the wildlife in their natural habitats, and to learn about nature conservation.

It is unusual to have a natural wildlife park right in the centre of a city.

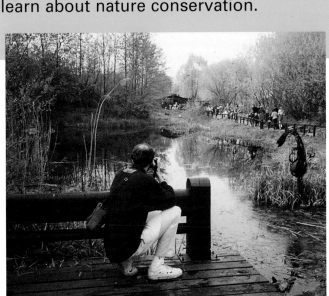

The pond is home to a great variety of plants and water creatures.

Working at home

Changing patterns of work are also starting to affect many types of settlements. In some countries, increasing numbers of people are working at home. They can use office machines such as computers and modems to link up with offices.

This way of working means that some people do not have to travel to city-centre offices every day. They can live in the country, but work for someone in a city a long way away. It also means that some businesses can move from towns to the country. They no longer have to be in urban areas to keep in touch with their customers. All this saves travelling and energy, and helps to reduce pollution.

Advances in technology mean that some people may not have to travel to an office each day.

Activity

Planning for the future

Make a plan of how your settlement may change in the future. Think about places for people to live, work and play, and the transport routes that link them.

- How do you think your settlement will change?
- How would *you* like it to change?
- How can you ensure that it is an environmentally friendly and attractive place to live?

Looking Ahead

Earth Summit and Agenda 21

In 1992 the world's leaders had a meeting to discuss the earth's environmental problems. The meeting was called the Earth Summit. The result of the meeting was a plan or programme for the twenty-first century, called Agenda 21. It is a plan to use the world's resources wisely and fairly to ensure a supply for everyone now and in the future. Each area is developing a Local Agenda 21, so people may care for their own environment.

How will people organize settlements in the future? We will have to use space, water and energy more wisely. We will still need green, open spaces if towns are to be pleasant places. Perhaps there will be more skyscrapers, or buildings underground, so that towns do not spread over the whole of the countryside. Whatever happens, we may have to change the way we design buildings and plan towns.

Overcrowding is just one of the environmental problems of cities.

Activity

Local Agenda 21

Find out what your town or village is doing about Agenda 21. For information, ask your local government office or town council. There should be a local Agenda 21 co-ordinator. He or she will be in charge of organizing services such as recycling, and helping everyone to decide how they want their home area to be.

What changes are planned and how can you play your part?

Ecolonia Town

Ecolonia is an area of 101 houses, built in 1991–92, near a town called Alphen aan den Rijn in the Netherlands. It was designed to show how a real settlement could be as environmentally friendly as possible.

Cars are allowed in but there are no through roads. People with cars are asked to park on the edge of the town, so that children, cyclists and walkers can use the streets safely.

Residents are encouraged to recycle every type of waste. Most of the houses have solar heating for water, and plenty of insulation to keep heat in. Some houses have filtered air that has been passed over waterfalls and through plants.

The houses are built around a small lake. Rain water runs into it, instead of into the sewage system. The lake has a reed bed that 'self-cleans' any dirty water that runs into it.

People in Ecolonia use the lake for boating and paddling.

Ecolonia has many visitors who come to see how it has been built and what it is like. Many of the features and ideas have been copied in other houses elsewhere in the Netherlands.

Glossary

Atmosphere   The gases surrounding the earth.

Commercial   To do with buying, selling and money.

Commuter   Someone who travels a long distance to and from daily work.

Congested   Crowded with people or traffic.

Conservation   Taking care of the environment to make sure that people, animals and plants always have everything they need to live.

Corps   A group of people doing the same activity.

Development   Gradual growth and change.

Environment   Everything in our surroundings: the earth, air and water.

Fumes   Smoke or gas that is harmful or that smells unpleasant.

Greenhouse gases   Gases which trap the sun's warmth near to the surface of the earth.

Habitat   The natural home of a plant or animal.

Industrial   Something involved with making or manufacturing goods, usually by machines in factories.

Logo   A small picture or letters used like a badge for an organization.

Nomad   Someone who does not live in one place, but who moves around.

Nuclear power Power released by a process called nuclear fission and used to make electricity.

Overcrowding   Too many people gathered together in one space.

Pollution   Damage to air, water or land by harmful materials.

Population   The number of people who live in a town, a country, or the world.

Port   The place where ships load or unload goods or people.

Recycle   To return used materials to be remade.

Redevelopment   Clearing a large area of a town or city and rebuilding.

Reservoir   An artificial lake made to store a large amount of water.

Resources   Things which humans use to survive or to improve their lives.

Rural   Belonging to the countryside.

Sewage   The liquid waste that is carried away, usually in pipes, from homes and factories.

Shelter   Something that protects from the weather, or danger.

Trade   Buying and selling goods or services.

Urban   Belonging to towns or cities.

Waste   Rubbish; things that are not needed or are unuseable.

Zone   An area that has special features.

Further Information

Topic Web — SETTLEMENTS

MUSIC
- Urban sounds: eg car horns, trains, industry
- 'Urban' music: eg hip-hop, rap, jazz

GEOGRAPHY
- Contrasting different type of settlements
- Land use
- Investigating an issue: eg out-of-town shops
- Environmental issues
- How people affect the environment
- Sustainability
- Mapwork

HISTORY
- Development of early settlements
- Growth of towns
- Life in town and country

ART & CRAFT
- View of settlements
- Drawings and models of future cities

DESIGN AND TECHNOLOGY
- House construction
- Design of settlements
- Use of materials

MATHS
- Collecting, recording, manipulating and interpreting data
- Simple statistics

SCIENCE
- Water cycle
- Waste disposal and recycling
- Energy production and use
- Environmental issues: eg habitat loss, water pollution, damage to ecosystems, conservation

ENGLISH
- Using settlements as a stimulus for creative writing
- Appropriate poetry
- Library skills

Further information

Books

Design and Make: Houses and Homes by John Williams, (Wayland 1997).
Exploring Materials series, (Wayland, 1993).
Forward in Geography: Settlement by May, Richardson and Waugh, (Nelson, 1997).
Natural Cycles: The Water Cycle by David Smith, (Wayland 1997).
Protecting our Planet: Waste, Recycling and Reuse by Steve Parker, (Wayland 1997).
Where I Live series, (Franklin Watts, 1993–94).

Multimedia

Data Bulletins: Exploring Cities, WWF, 1998.

Internet sites

Information on the Fort Lauderdale recycling programme can be found at:
http://info.ci.ftlaud.fl.us/citygov/depts/trash.htm

Places to visit

Bourton-on-the-Water, Cotswolds: traditional village with stream and model village.
Camley Street Natural Park, London.
Centre for Alternative Technology, Machynlleth, Wales: sustainable energy and waste disposal.
Chester, Cheshire: old city within Roman walls.
Docklands Light Railway, London: computerized train with good view of Docklands redevelopment.
Earth Centre, South Yorkshire: millenium project with large interactive visitor centre.
Falmouth, Cornwall: fishing port and holiday town on river estuary.
Lavenham, Suffolk: small town with medieval street pattern and many old buildings.
Letchworth Garden City, Hertfordshire: world's first garden city; planned town; heritage museum.
York, Yorkshire: old walled city with Minster; Castle Museum containing a Victorian street.

Index